DISCOVER!

EARTH AND SPACE SCIENCE

THE SOLAR SYSTEM

Beth Irving

Enslow PUBLISHING

Please visit our website, www.enslow.com. For a free color catalog of all our high-quality books, call toll free 1-800-398-2504 or fax 1-877-980-4454.

Cataloging-in-Publication Data
Names: Irving, Beth.
Title: The solar system / Beth Irving.
Description: Buffalo, NY : Enslow Publishing, 2027. | Series: Earth and space science | Includes glossary and index.
Identifiers: ISBN 9781978550353 (pbk.) | ISBN 9781978550360 (library bound) | ISBN 9781978550377 (ebook)
Subjects: LCSH: Solar system–Juvenile literature. | Planets–Juvenile literature. | Satellites–Juvenile literature. | Sun–Juvenile literature.
Classification: LCC QB501.3 I785 2027 | DDC 523.2–dc23

Published in 2027 by
Enslow Publishing
2544 Clinton Street
Buffalo, NY 14224

Designer: Claire Vanden Branden
Editor: Noah Riccardi

Photo Credits: Cover, p. 1 Sergey Nivens/Shutterstock.com; p. 5 AlexLMX/Shutterstock.com; p. 7 Dmitri T./Shutterstock.com; p. 9 Kabir9698/Shutterstock.com; p. 11 Vadim Sadovski/Shutterstock.com; pp. 13, 14, 18 buradaki/Shutterstock.com; p. 15 Artsiom P./Shutterstock.com; p. 17 24K-Production/Shutterstock.com; p. 19 Pzykodegoat/Shutterstock.com; p. 21 lovemushroom/Shutterstock.com.

Printed in China

CPSIA compliance information: Batch #QS27ENS: For further information contact Enslow Publishing, at 1-800-398-2504.

CONTENTS

BOLDFACE WORDS APPEAR IN THE GLOSSARY.

A SPACE NEIGHBORHOOD

Our solar system is like a big **neighborhood** in space. It includes the sun and many space objects that move around the sun.

Earth is a planet. Planets are large bodies in our solar system that move around the sun. Each planet has its own path around the sun. This path is called its **orbit**.

The sun is a star, just like stars in the night sky. But the sun is much closer to us. It's made of different gases. These gases are very hot. The sun is much larger than the planets.

The inner planets are the ones closest to the sun. There are four inner planets. They are Mercury, Venus, Earth, and Mars. They're all made up of rock.

The outer planets are farther away from the sun. They're larger than the inner planets and are made of gas. The outer planets are Jupiter, Saturn, Uranus, and Neptune.

Many planets have smaller bodies that orbit them. These are called moons. Earth has one moon that you can see in the sky.

Some space objects that orbit the sun are too small to be called planets. These objects are known as **dwarf planets**. Pluto is one of these.

Asteroids are large space rocks that also orbit the sun. Many asteroids orbit in the asteroid belt. This area is between the inner and outer planets.

MERCURY TO MARS

Mercury is closest to the sun. It travels around the sun quickly. It makes one orbit in just 88 days. Earth takes a whole year to make one orbit!

Venus is second closest to the sun. It's too hot for things to live there. Venus has many openings in the ground called volcanoes. Hot gases and **melted** rock come out of them.

Planet Earth is our home. It's the third planet from the sun. Earth is the only planet where we know things can live. There's a lot of water on Earth.

Mars is the next planet. We call it the Red Planet because its **soil** is red. Scientists have sent robots to explore its surface.

JUPITER TO NEPTUNE

The outer planets are sometimes called gas giants. Jupiter is the first gas giant. It's the largest planet in our solar system. It has a storm called the Great Red Spot. It has been going on for 300 years.

Saturn is the second largest planet in the solar system. It's known for the many icy rings that go around it.

The seventh planet in our solar system is Uranus. It's made of gases that give it a blue color. Uranus has rings, too. It has 11 of them.

The last planet is Neptune. It's the farthest planet from the sun and has the longest orbit. Neptune is made of gases, too. Its gases also make it look blue.

LOOK UP!

We can see planets like Venus and Mars in the night sky with our eyes. People can also use **spacecraft** to study the other planets.

It's fun to explore our solar system! There are many great things to discover about space. Would you like to be a space explorer when you grow up?

GLOSSARY

dwarf planets: Nearly-round space objects too small to be planets.
melted: Made soft and flowing because of heat.
neighborhood: An area of things close to one another.
orbit: To move in a circle around something; also, the path of an object flying in a circle around something.
soil: Dirt.
spacecraft: Ships that people send up into outer space.

FOR MORE INFORMATION

Books

Andrews, Elizabeth. *Planets*. Minneapolis, MN: Abdo Publishing, 2025.

Wood, Alix. *Blast Off to Other Planets*. Buffalo, NY: Rosen Publishing, 2025.

Websites

Britannica Kids: Solar System
kids.britannica.com/kids/article/solar-system/353789
Learn more about the solar system at this site.

National Geographic Kids: Passport to Space
kids.nationalgeographic.com/space
Learn more about outer space at this website.

Publisher's note to educators and parents: Our editors have carefully reviewed these websites to ensure that they are suitable for students. Many websites change frequently, however, and we cannot guarantee that a site's future contents will continue to meet our high standards of quality and educational value. Be advised that students should be closely supervised whenever they access the internet.

INDEX